The Amazing Life of
BENJAMIN FRANKLIN

Also by JAMES CROSS GIBLIN
Illustrated by MICHAEL DOOLING

George Washington
A PICTURE BOOK BIOGRAPHY

Thomas Jefferson
A PICTURE BOOK BIOGRAPHY

The Amazing Life of BENJAMIN FRANKLIN

by JAMES CROSS GIBLIN ❧ illustrated by MICHAEL DOOLING

SCHOLASTIC PAPERBACK NONFICTION

Library of Congress Cataloging-in-Publication Data available.

ISBN-13: 978-0-439-81065-4
ISBN-10: 0-439-81065-5

12 11 10 9 14 15/0

Printed in the U.S.A. 40

First Scholastic paperback printing, January 2006

Book design by David Caplan
The display type was set in Aqualine.
The text type was set in 12-point Hoefler Text-Roman.
The artwork was rendered in oil on canvas.

The use of initial caps, uneven word spacing, and double columns is meant
to graphically echo Franklin's newspaper, *The Pennsylvania Gazette*.

Special thanks to Roy E. Goodman, Curator of Printed Materials at the American Philosophical
Society, for fact-checking the text and art. And to Patia Kubel from Ben Franklin's Printing Office
and Bindery for her help in fact-checking the artist's note.

For Jim Murphy, colleague and friend

—J.C.G.

To Jane

—M.D.

WHEN BENJAMIN FRANKLIN WAS A BOY, there were often thirteen or more people crowded around the family dining table. Ben was one of seventeen children, and the youngest of ten sons. Many of his older brothers and sisters still took their meals at home.

Home was a house on Milk Street in Boston, Massachusetts, where Ben had been born in 1706. He loved the bustle and excitement of Boston — the shops filled with all sorts of goods, the wharves jammed with ships ready to sail to the far corners of the world.

He dreamed of going to sea himself one day, but there wasn't much chance of that. With so many mouths to feed, Ben's father needed him to help out. And so, after just two years of schooling, ten-year-old Ben went to work in Mr. Franklin's candle-and-soap-making shop.

Ben hated shaping wicks for the candles and stirring the boiling tallow for the soap. At last, after two years, his father took pity on the boy and sought another profession for him. But what would it be? Ben wasn't interested in becoming a bricklayer, a carpenter, or a roofer. He still wanted to go to sea.

Then Mr. Franklin had an idea. Ben was smart. He loved to read and was a good speller. Maybe he'd like to go to work for his older brother James, who was a printer.

The idea appealed to Ben — but not the pledge his father signed. The pledge said Ben would have to serve as an apprentice to his brother, without pay, for nine years. He wouldn't be free until he was twenty-one.

♦ Ben Franklin's Father ♦

Once he got started, Ben enjoyed working in the printing shop. He learned how to set type and operate the heavy wooden press. At night and before the shop opened in the morning, he read book after book that he borrowed from nearby bookstores.

Soon he started to write himself. He began with poems, but switched to prose pieces after his father told him, "Verse-makers are always beggars."

To improve his writing style, he would read an article in a magazine, put it aside for a few days, and then rewrite the article from memory. Then he would compare what he had done with the original. He found that this exercise helped him to correct his faults. It also increased his vocabulary.

In 1721, Ben's brother James decided to start a newspaper, the *New England Courant*. He invited readers to send in articles, so Ben wrote a humorous piece and signed it with a girl's name, Silence Dogood. He was afraid his brother wouldn't print the article if he knew Ben had written it. The article was so popular that Ben wrote thirteen more.

Later, his brother got in trouble with the Boston city council for publishing articles that made fun of the Puritan church. James was told he couldn't run his paper anymore, but he thought of a way around the order. He freed seventeen-year-old Ben from his apprenticeship and made him the editor.

Ben liked his new job and his new freedom. He often quarreled with his brother, though. At last Ben decided to look for a job in another printing shop, but his angry brother kept other printers in Boston from hiring him. There was only one thing Ben could do — leave Boston and seek work elsewhere.

• Young Ben Franklin •

Without telling anyone, he sold some books to raise money and bought passage on a boat to New York. The trip took three days but was still faster than going by horse and carriage. Many of the roads then were little more than dirt paths.

Ben couldn't find a job in New York. But he heard of one in Philadelphia, so he traveled there by boat and on foot. It turned out to be a five-day journey. He had to walk fifty miles across New Jersey in heavy rain, and he spent several nights in cheap roadside inns.

When Ben finally arrived in Philadelphia, he was hungry, tired, and dirty. He brushed off his clothes as best he could, bought some rolls with a threepenny piece, and rented a bed in a lodging house. The next day he called on the printer he had heard about and was hired on the spot. Thus began Benjamin Franklin's life and career in Philadelphia, the city he would always think of as home.

Ben soon proved his worth as a printer. Although he was only eighteen, he made plans to open his own shop. He decided to travel all the way to London, England, to buy the presses and type he would need for the business. In 1724, America was still a colony of England and was not allowed to manufacture items like printing presses. All such goods had to be imported from the mother country.

There were no steamships then, let alone airplanes, so it took Ben more than two months to cross the Atlantic in a sailing ship. Fortunately the ship escaped being attacked by pirates. When he got to London at last, Ben discovered that the letter of credit he needed to pay for the presses and type had not come through. Almost penniless and thousands of miles from home, he didn't know what he would do.

Ben was always optimistic, though. He found work with a London printer and spent his free time exploring the great city and reading all the latest books. He had his share of fun, too, going to pubs with his friends and flirting with the pretty girls he met.

Whatever he did, he felt proud to be living in London. It was the heart of the vast British Empire, of which America was just one small part. But after eighteen months Ben began to be homesick for his native land. When a merchant visiting London offered him a job back in Philadelphia, he accepted at once.

On his return home, Ben first worked for the merchant, then got his old job back at the printing shop. Before long he was able to buy out his employer and take over the business. In the meantime, he had helped to found the Junto, a club of bright young men who were interested in books and learning.

He also courted and married a young widow, Deborah Read. Deborah could barely read and write, but she was steady and loyal and had a good head for business. Ben was devoted to her. He called her "My dear child," and she called him "Pappy." Besides keeping house, she helped him manage the printing shop and the store he opened next to it. In the store, they sold stationery, pens, ink, candles, and books.

Soon after Ben and Deborah were married, a son, William, entered the Franklin household. Later the Franklins had two other children, a son, Francis, and a daughter, Sarah. Francis — known as Franky — was the joy of his father's life. When the little boy died of smallpox at the age of four, Ben grieved for months.

Now that his printing business was a success, Ben decided to start a weekly newspaper, *The Pennsylvania Gazette*. Then he launched the annual publication that made him famous, *Poor Richard's Almanack*. The *Almanack* contained a calendar, weather forecasts for the year, poems, and sayings. Ben wrote much of the *Almanack* himself, and he made sure there was plenty of humor in it. Within a few years, each edition was selling 10,000 copies — a huge sale in colonial America.

As Ben became more prosperous, he turned his attention to things that would make Philadelphia a better place to live. With the Junto members and other friends, he helped to establish the first library in the colonies. He and the Junto went on to help found Philadelphia's first fire department, made up of thirty volunteer firemen. They pressed the city government to pave and light the city's muddy streets, and to clean them regularly.

THE
Pennsylvania GAZETTE
Containing the freshest Advices Foreign and Domestick

Ben urged the city to set up an academy for the education of its young people. At the same time, he said a free school should be opened for the instruction of poor children who could not afford to attend the academy.

He also supported the establishment of Philadelphia's first hospital "for the relief of the sick and miserable." One floor would be reserved for the treatment of the mentally ill, "there being no other place in which they might be confined and subjected to proper management for their recovery."

Ben worked hard to bring about all these civic improvements. He served on countless committees and wrote one newspaper article after another. But he always played down his own role in the proceedings. For he had learned that people were more likely to endorse something new if they thought it was their idea.

By the age of forty-two, Ben had made enough money to retire from the printing business. Now he could devote all of his time and energy to public affairs and to a new interest — science. He had become intrigued with electricity, about which little was known at the time. No one had yet figured out how to harness electricity as a source of power. There were no electric appliances. There weren't even any electric lights.

Ben guessed that electricity and lightning were one and the same. But how could he prove it? With his son, William, he devised an

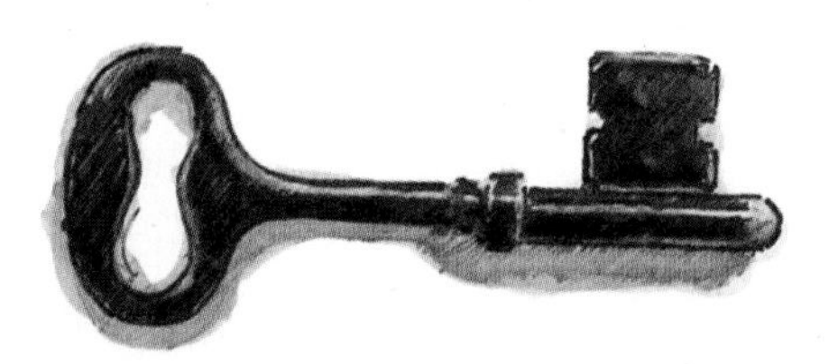

experiment that used a kite to draw lightning down from a stormy June sky. The lightning raced along a rope attached to the tail of the kite and electrified a metal key at the rope's end.

When Ben got a shock from the key, he had his proof. He made practical use of it by inventing the lightning rod. A pointed metal rod on top of a building would attract the dangerous bolts of lightning. They would flow down a wire outside the building and sink harmlessly into the ground. In this way, the building would be protected from damage by lightning.

Ben refused to patent his invention or to profit from it in any way. Instead he published a detailed description of his lightning rod so that people everywhere could benefit from it.

While he was experimenting with lightning, Ben was elected to the Pennsylvania Assembly. The assembly helped to govern the colony. Soon after that, in 1753, he was named Deputy Postmaster General for the six northern colonies. These new public duties left him little time for science, so he put it aside for the moment.

When Ben started work with the postal service, it took six weeks for a letter to travel the 304 miles between Boston and Philadelphia. Ben cut the time down to three weeks by employing more relay riders and using better and more direct roads. He also started the first deliveries of mail in Philadelphia. Before that, people had to go to the post office to pick up their mail.

• Post Rider •

In 1754, trouble developed on America's western frontier. The French and their Indian allies swept down from Canada to lay claim to the Ohio River Valley. It looked as if they might move on east into Pennsylvania and New York. A conference was hastily arranged in Albany, New York, to deal with the problem.

Benjamin Franklin took part in the conference and offered a bold new plan for the defense of the colonies. He proposed that the northern colonies unite for their mutual benefit. He also urged that two new colonies be established in the Ohio Territory to prevent the French and their allies from moving east.

This was the first time anyone had suggested that the American colonies unite and that they expand westward. But Ben wasn't calling for America to be independent from Great Britain — far from it. He was still proud to be a citizen of the British Empire. And he believed his plan for union would make America a stronger part of the Empire.

At first there was a lot of support for Ben's plan. But gradually it faded away. The colonies feared they would lose some of their power and freedom of action if they joined forces. As a result, the idea of a united America vanished from people's minds — for the time being.

Pennsylvania, like the other colonies, was responsible for its own defense. But the powerful Penn family refused to pay its fair share of the taxes needed to maintain a strong militia. Ben and the other members of the Pennsylvania Assembly tried to get the Penns to change their minds, but they could not be budged. Their ancestor, William Penn, had founded the colony, and the family continued to rule it from England under a charter from the king.

The assembly decided there was only one thing to do — send Benjamin Franklin to England to act as its agent. Maybe he could get the British government to set aside the Penns' charter and take over control of the Pennsylvania colony. If not that, the British could at least make the Penns pay taxes on their vast landholdings.

Ben agreed to go and wanted his wife and his son, William, to accompany him. Twenty-six-year-old William was eager to make the trip. But Deborah Franklin wouldn't even consider it. She told Ben the very thought of the long ocean voyage terrified her. And so, on June 20, 1757, Ben set sail for England without his beloved wife.

• William Penn •

Ben was surprised at how much London had grown in the thirty-two years since he was last there. He and William rented four rooms in the home of a widow, and Ben set up his electrical equipment in one of the rooms. William enrolled in a university and began to study law.

For exercise, Ben went swimming in the Thames River. And first thing every morning he took an air bath. He opened the windows in his bedroom, took off his nightshirt, and let the warm or cold breezes blow over his body. Many people of the time thought fresh air was dangerous, but not Ben!

His fellow scientists welcomed Ben to London. They had heard of his experiments with electricity and held him in high esteem. But the Penn family was not happy that he had come. For three years they stubbornly resisted all his arguments that their estates in Pennsylvania should be taxed. Ben waited patiently, however, and at last the Penns agreed to pay some taxes on their properties.

His mission accomplished, Ben could have returned to America at this point. But he had a good reason for staying on in England. There was a chance that his son, William, might be named the new royal governor of New Jersey. Ben wanted to do everything he could to help William obtain the post.

In the summer of 1762 William was appointed, and father and son made plans to return home at once. Ben had been in London for five years, and he hated to leave his English friends. But he was eager to see his wife, Deborah, and their daughter, Sarah, who was known as Sally. Sally had grown into an attractive young woman while he was away.

Back in America, Ben looked on proudly when William was installed as the royal governor of New Jersey in February 1763. Conditions in the colonies were not calm, however. Indian raids on frontier settlements had become more frequent. And the political situation in England, where a new king had come to the throne, was extremely confusing. Once again the Pennsylvania Assembly asked Ben to go to London to represent America's interests.

Ben was reluctant. He knew his wife would never agree to accompany him, and he dreaded going alone. Besides, he was fifty-six, which was considered old at the time. This long journey might well prove to be his last. On the other hand, he felt he was needed in London. And so in the end he accepted the assignment. Three hundred friends and admirers saw him off when he sailed for England on November 9, 1764.

♦ Deborah Franklin ♦

When he arrived in London a month later, Ben was horrified to learn that the British government was about to pass the Stamp Act. The act would require that Americans pay a fee to have a royal stamp put on all their legal documents, from marriage licenses to wills.

Americans had paid many taxes to Great Britain before, but the taxes had always been levied by the colonists themselves. This would be the first time Americans had to pay a tax levied on them by the British government. Ben knew his fellow Americans would be angry when they heard of the tax. He worried that their protests might turn violent.

He was right. There were riots in Boston, Newport, and New Haven. Mobs attacked the homes of tax collectors and threatened to tar and feather them.

When he heard of these incidents, Ben vowed to do everything he could to get the Stamp Act repealed. If it weren't, he was afraid there might be a serious break between the colonies and Great Britain. But he still believed firmly that such a break could be avoided. He still wanted America to be a part of the British Empire.

On February 13, 1766, Ben appeared in person before the British House of Commons to answer the members' questions. Most of the members were dressed in the latest fashions and had white wigs on their heads. Ben wore a simple brown suit and his wig wasn't as stylish as the others. He didn't care. He was there to represent America, not show off his clothes.

One of the members asked him, "If the Stamp Act is not repealed, what do you think will be the consequences?"

"A total loss of the respect and affection the people of America bear to this country," Ben replied. He said they might show their lack of respect by refusing to buy British goods.

Some of the members who listened to Ben were sympathetic to the Americans. Other members were all for the Stamp Act. They thought Britain should impose any taxes it wanted on the colonies. But a majority of the members feared Britain's trade with the colonies would suffer if the act remained in effect. They voted to repeal it.

Ben was delighted, but soon a new problem arose. Those in favor of taxing the colonies levied extra duties on glass, paint, paper, tea, and other products the colonies had to import from Britain.

Crowds rioted again in Boston and other places to protest the new taxes. For the first time, Ben began to have doubts about America's future within the Empire. He hated to admit it, but perhaps America would soon have to go its own way.

Responding to the protests, the British removed all of the new taxes except for the one on tea. Ben was encouraged, but he knew Britain's position hadn't really changed. Nor had the Americans' response to it. He wrote a humorous song about the situation:

We have an old mother
that peevish is grown
She snubs us like children
that scarce walk alone
She forgets we've grown up
and have sense of our own
Which nobody can deny, deny
Which nobody can deny.

But Ben's son, William, was still trying to deny it. As the royal governor of New Jersey, he loyally supported the British position. This disappointed Ben, but he realized he could not change his son's mind. Then came an event that set America firmly on the road toward revolution. It would also have a deep and lasting effect on Benjamin Franklin.

On the night of December 16, 1773, a mob of fifty or so citizens of Boston disguised themselves as Indians and stormed aboard three British ships docked in the harbor. They dumped 300 chests of tea into the salt water in a protest against the hated tax on tea. This was the event that soon became known as the Boston Tea Party.

When word of the dumping reached England in January 1774, the reaction was swift and furious. Ben was summoned to appear before the government's Privy Council. By now he was representing three colonies in London besides Pennsylvania: Georgia, New Jersey, and Massachusetts.

For over an hour Ben stood silently in the council chamber while those who had dumped the tea were denounced. The council members thought the protesters were entirely to blame for the incident. They would not even listen to the idea that the tax on tea might have had something to do with it.

The council punished Boston by closing its port to traffic until the destroyed tea was paid for. And they punished Ben by dismissing him from his job as Deputy Postmaster General for the colonies. Their moves shook his hopes that some sort of compromise could still be reached between America and Great Britain.

Ben was pleased that the other colonies rallied around Massachusetts at this difficult time. He was even more pleased when the colonies decided to meet in Philadelphia to discuss a common approach to the crisis. But he worried about his relationship with his son. William took the British side as usual, and told Ben that he thought the Massachusetts colonists were in the wrong.

The Philadelphia meeting — which was known as the First Continental Congress — sent a petition to Parliament. The petition listed all the wrongs the British government had done to the colonies and asked for relief. Ben and his British friends spoke out in favor of the petition, but Parliament refused even to consider it.

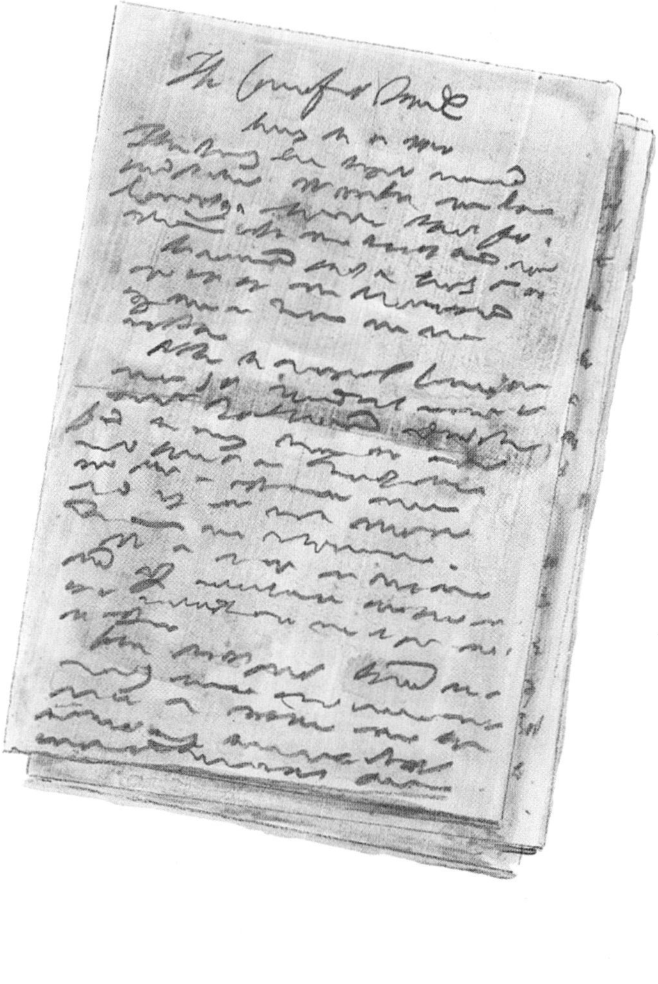

Their refusal saddened Ben. He was made even sadder a few days later when a letter arrived from his son, William. The letter said that Ben's wife, Deborah, had died of a stroke a month earlier, on December 19, 1774. William wrote that he had struggled through deep snowdrifts to attend her funeral in Philadelphia.

For some time Ben had been thinking he should go home to America. It had been ten years since he had seen his wife. The strained relations between Britain and America had made him stay in London, however. Now it was too late — Deborah was gone.

But he still had his properties in America to look after. He also felt his situation in England was getting dangerous. "If by some accident the British troops and the people of New England come to blows, I should probably be arrested," he wrote a friend. And so he made plans to leave England as soon as possible.

On the long voyage home, Ben was filled with worries. He had tried hard to keep America and Britain together, but he had failed. Now a war between them seemed inevitable. Ben had no doubts where he would stand in the conflict. Much as he loved England, he was first of all an American. But which side would his son, the royal governor, choose?

♦ William Franklin ♦

When his ship landed, Ben heard the news he had dreaded most. Two weeks earlier, on April 19, 1775, fighting had broken out in Lexington, Massachusetts, between British soldiers and American militiamen. The Revolutionary War — the war Ben Franklin had tried with all his might to prevent — had begun.

• Sarah Franklin Bache •

Ben was greeted in Philadelphia by his daughter, Sarah, her husband, Richard Bache, and their three sons. He had no time for a rest, however. The Second Continental Congress was about to begin, and Ben was asked to serve as a delegate. The congress decided simply to send another petition to King George. It wasn't ready yet to demand independence from Great Britain.

Ben also met with his son, William, at a friend's estate. William was shocked that his father now believed America should be independent. The younger Franklin wanted America to remain in the Empire. And he wanted to keep his job as governor of New Jersey.

George Washington had gone to Massachusetts as commander of the new American army. Ben traveled to Massachusetts to offer Washington his advice and support. At the time, it was estimated that about one-third of the colonists were for independence, one-third were opposed, and the rest didn't care one way or the other.

Many of those opposed to independence changed their minds after King George forbade all trade with the colonies. The king also said British ships could now seize any American vessels they met on the high seas.

Congress reacted to the king's moves by opening American ports to the ships of all nations except those of Great Britain. It went on to tell the American people they should no longer support the British government in any way.

Ben was in favor of these congressional actions, but William Franklin denounced them. Rather than obey orders, he tried to get the New Jersey Assembly to arrange a separate peace with Great Britain.

The assembly refused to do so. Instead it cut off Governor Franklin's salary and put him under house arrest. He wouldn't stay in his home, however, so the assembly had him transported to a prison in Connecticut. A sorrowful Ben made no move to contact his son or to help him.

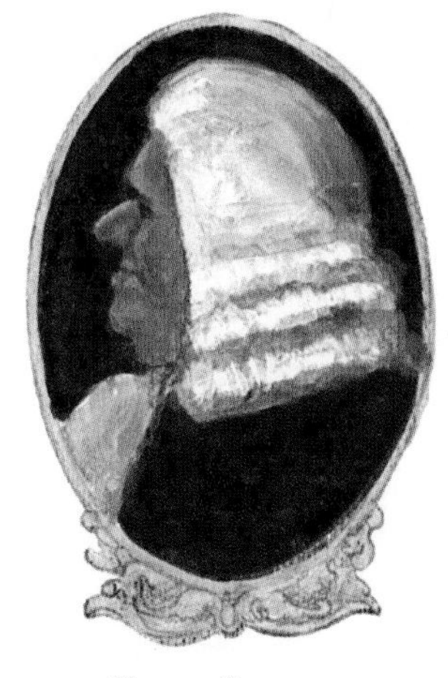

• King George •

On June 7, 1776, a resolution was finally introduced in Congress that the colonies should be "free and independent states." A committee was formed to write a declaration of independence, and Ben was named to it. But because of his son's behavior, he wasn't asked to draft the declaration. Thomas Jefferson got the assignment instead. Ben did suggest a few changes in the declaration, and he signed it along with the other members of Congress on August 7, 1776.

Meanwhile, George Washington's army was having a hard time in New York. They lost the Battle of Long Island and were forced to withdraw first to Manhattan, and then to New Jersey. But Ben stood firm when he met with a British lord who had come to America to try to work out a peace treaty. "America can never return to the domination of Britain," Franklin said.

At this moment, an offer of help came from an unexpected place. France had long been an enemy of Great Britain. Now the French government let Congress know that it was sympathetic to America's desire for independence. It might even be willing to aid America in its war with Britain.

Congress decided to send representatives to France to explore ways America and France could cooperate. The members unanimously chose seventy-year-old Benjamin Franklin to be the chief representative.

Ben was well aware of the dangers of a winter voyage across the Atlantic in wartime. The waters were full of British cruisers, and their captains would be sure to hang Franklin as a traitor if they captured his ship. But at his age, few things frightened Ben. He sailed for France in November 1776, and arrived safely four weeks later. Strong winds helped his ship make better time than usual.

Ben was welcomed warmly in Paris by government officials, scientists, and the common people. They remembered Poor Richard, the character he had created in his famous *Almanack*, and gave Ben the nickname "Bon Homme Richard," meaning "Good Man Richard."

• George Washington •

• Thomas Jefferson •

Over the next few years, the Revolutionary War raged back and forth in America, with the British winning one battle and the Americans the next. At the same time, Ben worked day and night in France to win support for George Washington's army. He managed to obtain large loans with which the army could buy badly needed weapons and supplies.

In 1778, Ben worked out the final terms of a military alliance between France and America. Now he became even better known in France. He didn't let it go to his head, though. In a letter to his sister, he wrote: "The vogue I am in here has occasioned so many paintings, busts, medals & prints to be made of me, and distributed throughout the kingdom, that my face is now almost as well known as the moon. But," he added, "one is not to expect being always in fashion."

At seventy-two, Ben still had an eye for the ladies. He even fell in love with one, Madame Helvétius. She was a brilliant widow who entertained all the leading writers, scientists, and politicians in her home. Ben went so far as to propose marriage, but the widow wasn't ready for that. However, she remained a good friend for the rest of his life.

Distressing news about his son, William, reached Ben in 1780. William had been exchanged for an American prisoner-of-war, and had gone to British-held New York. There he joined a band of guerrilla fighters who launched raids against their fellow Americans in New Jersey, New York, and Connecticut. Innocent people had been wounded and killed in the raids.

Ben was furious when he heard what William had done. It was one thing to support Britain in the war, another to engage in sneak attacks on his own people.

Earlier, Ben had hoped he and his son might find some way to get together again. Now he doubted whether that would ever be possible.

Better news came from America in November 1781. General George Washington, with the help of a French force, had trapped the best British army group in America at Yorktown in Virginia. More than 8,000 British soldiers and their commander, Lord Cornwallis, had been taken prisoner. The Revolutionary War dragged on, but never again did the British have a chance of winning it.

• Madame Helvétius •

• Benjamin Franklin •

In Paris, Benjamin Franklin let it be known that he was authorized to discuss a peace treaty with Great Britain when King George was ready. During 1782, Ben and the other American representatives, John Adams and John Jay, thrashed out the terms of the treaty. It guaranteed full and complete independence for America, and the withdrawal of all British troops from its territory.

The British pressed hard for payments to be made to British loyalists whose American properties had been seized during the Revolution. Ben was dead set against this. His son, William, had fled to England and was now pleading the cause of the loyalists before Parliament. Ben didn't want William and others like him to be rewarded in any way.

The final peace treaty between Great Britain and the young United States was signed on September 3, 1783. In the meantime, Ben had found a new scientific interest — ballooning.

The French had begun filling large silk balloons with heated air or hydrogen gas, and then sending them aloft. Cabins carrying human passengers were attached to some of the balloons. They rose to heights of 500 feet or more. Ben delighted in watching these balloon experiments, and when someone wondered what good they did, he replied, "What good is a newborn baby?"

With the peace treaty signed, Ben decided it was time for him to go home. He was seventy-eight now, and ready to retire at last. While he was making plans for his departure, a letter arrived from his son. William said he wanted to renew their relationship and would like to come to Paris to see Ben. But William did not admit that any of his actions during the war had been wrong.

Ben wrote back at once to say that he, too, would like to resume relations.

However, now would not be a good time for William to visit Paris. And then Ben expressed his deepest feelings to William: "Nothing has ever hurt me so much as to find myself deserted in my old age by my only son; and not only deserted, but to find him taking up arms against me, in a cause wherein my good fame, fortune, and life were all at stake."

As soon as Congress accepted his resignation, Ben got ready to leave France. He liked the man who had been named to succeed him as ambassador: Thomas Jefferson.

For some time, Ben had suffered from gallstones. By now they had gotten so painful that he could not travel by jolting carriage. So King Louis XVI lent him a royal litter for the journey from Paris to the coast. All his friends gathered on a July day in 1785 to see him off.

Ben's ship stopped briefly at Southampton, England, on its way to America. William came down from London to see him there, hoping they could get on friendly terms again. But that didn't happen. Their conversation turned into a cold discussion of family business matters, and they parted without any show of affection. It would be Ben's last meeting with his son.

• King Louis XVI •

An enormous crowd greeted Ben on his return to Philadelphia. "God be praised and thanked for all His mercies," he wrote about the welcome in his travel diary.

Ben looked forward to spending the rest of his days in leisure, working on his autobiography, and making scientific investigations. Instead, he soon found himself involved in politics once more.

The Articles of Confederation, which the states had signed in the early days of the Revolution, were too weak to bind the new nation together. Congress decided to hold a convention to draft a new and stronger constitution for the United States. And Ben Franklin, at age eighty-one, was asked to serve as a delegate to the convention.

Almost daily in the summer of 1787, Ben trudged from his house to the Pennsylvania State House. There he spent long hours trying to balance the needs of poor states and rich states, large states and small states, slave states and free states.

It was Ben who suggested that there be two houses of Congress under the new Constitution. In the Senate, all the states would have equal representation. In the House of Representatives, the number of representatives each state had would depend on how many people lived in the state. The bigger the population, the greater the number of representatives. Ben's suggestion passed by a narrow margin — five to four, with one state divided.

As the convention came to a close, the delegates feared that not enough states would ratify the Constitution for it to become law. They asked Ben to speak out in favor of the Constitution because they knew people would listen to him.

His gallstones were giving him so much pain that Ben found it difficult to stand. Another delegate read his speech for him. In it, Ben said he "did not entirely approve of this Constitution," but he felt it was the best that could be achieved. He urged all the states to endorse it. A majority of states agreed with him, and the Constitution became law in June 1788. It is still in effect today, more than two hundred years later.

Ben was delighted to hear that the Constitution had been adopted. But he was too old and ill, he said, to take any part in enforcing it. Instead, he strongly backed George Washington as the first president of the United States.

By now, Ben was in almost constant pain from his gallstones. There were lots of people to help him forget the pain, though. His daughter, Sarah, her husband, and their seven children had moved in with him. His house was almost as crowded and lively as the one he had grown up in.

In spite of his ailments, Ben took on one last public service job. He agreed to be the president of a group that urged the end of slavery in the United States.

The group presented its petition to the new Congress, but it was immediately rejected. A senator from the slave state of Georgia led the attack against it. He claimed that blacks were better off and happier as slaves. Not until the Civil War, more than seventy-five years later, would slavery finally be abolished in the United States.

Early in 1790, Ben's health took a turn for the worse. His daughter told him she was praying he would get better and live longer. But Ben, who was now in pain day and night, replied honestly, "I hope not." A few hours later, on April 17, 1790, the eighty-four-year-old Benjamin Franklin passed away peacefully.

In the years after his death, Franklin would be remembered for many things. The wit and wisdom of *Poor Richard's Almanack*. The libraries, schools, and hospitals he founded. His experiments with electricity and his useful inventions.

Above all, he would be honored for the role he played in helping America win its freedom, and then in writing the Constitution. He had proved himself a true patriot — even though it meant losing the love and respect of his only living son.

Because of his many talents and skills, Ben Franklin has often been called the "wisest American." He offered a humbler description in the epitaph he wrote for his gravestone. Remembering where he had started, he called himself simply: *B Franklin Printer*.

Important Dates
FROM BENJAMIN FRANKLIN'S LIFE

January 17, 1706 — Benjamin Franklin is born in Boston, Massachusetts.

1716 — At age ten, Ben goes to work in his father's candle-and-soap-making shop.

1718 — Ben is apprenticed to his older brother James, a printer.

April 2, 1722 — Sixteen-year-old Ben's first humorous article is published in his brother's newspaper.

September 1723 — Ben leaves Boston to find work elsewhere and gets a job with a printer in Philadelphia.

November 1724 — Eighteen-year-old Ben sails across the Atlantic to London, England, and finds work as a printer there.

July 23, 1726 — A homesick Ben leaves London and sets sail for Philadelphia.

February 1728 — Ben opens his own printing business in Philadelphia.

December 1728 — Ben starts a newspaper, *The Pennsylvania Gazette*, which he edits as well as prints. He also writes many of the articles.

September 1, 1730 — Ben marries Deborah Read.

Late 1730 — Ben's son William is born.

October 20, 1732 — Another son, Francis Folger Franklin, is born.

December 1732 — The first edition of *Poor Richard's Almanack* is published.

November 21, 1736 — Francis (Franky) Franklin dies of smallpox at age four.

September 11, 1743 — Ben's only daughter, Sarah, is born.

September 1748 — Ben retires from his printing business and spends much of his time on scientific experiments.

August 1751 — Ben is elected to serve in the Pennsylvania Assembly.

June 1752 — Ben flies a kite in a thunderstorm and proves that lightning and electricity are one and the same.

September 1752 — Ben invents the lightning rod.

August 10, 1753 — Ben is appointed Deputy Postmaster General for the northern colonies.

July 1754 — At a conference in Albany, New York, Ben offers a plan to unite the colonies.

June 20, 1757 — Ben and his son, William, set sail for England, where Ben will be Pennsylvania's representative in London.

Summer 1762 — Ben and William return to America.

February 1763 — William is installed as the royal governor of New Jersey.

November, 1764 — Ben goes back once again to London.

December 19, 1774 — Ben's wife, Deborah, dies in Philadelphia at age sixty-six.

April 1775 — Ben returns to America.

April 19, 1775 — Fighting breaks out in Lexington, Massachusetts, between British soldiers and American militiamen. The Revolutionary War has begun.

July 4, 1776 — Congress issues the Declaration of Independence.

November 1776 — Benjamin Franklin sails to France to represent the new United States in Paris.

1780 — William Franklin, who has remained loyal to Britain, takes part in guerrilla raids on his fellow Americans.

November 1781 — General George Washington wins a decisive victory over the British at Yorktown in Virginia.

1783 — Ben helps to negotiate the peace treaty between the United States and Great Britain. It is signed on September 3.

September 1785 — Ben returns to his home in Philadelphia for the last time.

Summer 1787 — The eighty-one-year-old Ben is a delegate to the convention that writes the U.S. Constitution.

April 17, 1790 — Benjamin Franklin dies in Philadelphia at the age of eighty-four.

Benjamin Franklin
THE INVENTOR

Besides the lightning rod, Benjamin Franklin invented or improved many other useful things during his long life. Here are a few of them.

The Pennsylvanian Fireplace
(also known as the Franklin Stove)

In Franklin's day, most homes, schools, offices, and stores were heated by wood fires that blazed in open fireplaces. This method of heating was very inefficient. Much of the warm air went up the chimney, while smoke from the fire often came out into the room.

Ben invented a new kind of stove that solved both these problems. It could be installed in any fireplace and spread hot air evenly throughout the room. At the same time, it funneled the smoke away from the room and up the chimney.

Because very little heat was lost, the Franklin stove required less wood than an ordinary fireplace. This helped families to save on fuel costs, especially in the northern colonies where cold weather usually arrived in October and stayed until April.

A New Kind of Clock

Ben was the first American to devise a clock with three wheels that showed the hours, the minutes, and the seconds. Clocks up till then showed only the hours and minutes.

An Artificial Arm

In the store that Ben and his wife ran next to his printing shop, shelves went all the way up to the ceiling. Ben needed something to help him get items from the topmost shelves. So he invented an "artificial arm" — a long pole with a pair of pincers at the end. The person holding the pole could grasp the desired item with the pincers and lift it down quickly and easily.

A Library Chair

Ben often used the artificial arm to reach books on the top shelves of his home library. He also designed what he called his library chair. When the seat was pulled up, steps were revealed beneath it. Ben climbed up on the steps to get a book he wanted from a high shelf.

Security Mirrors

Security was as much of a concern in colonial America as in our cities and suburbs today. To help deal with this problem, Ben thought of a way a homeowner could see who was at the front door before he opened it. He put one mirror above the door, positioned so that it would reflect the person standing below. Then he placed a second mirror in a window next to the door to catch the reflection from the first mirror. Ben's invention became so popular in his home city that it was nicknamed the "Philadelphia Busybody."

Bifocal Glasses

As he grew older, Ben had to have two pairs of glasses — one for reading, the other for seeing things at a distance. This was inconvenient; often he didn't have the right pair with him when he needed it. At last Ben went to a lens maker in Paris, where he was living at the time. He told the man he wanted to have "the lenses cut, and half of each lens put in the same frame. By this means — as I wear my spectacles constantly — I will have only to move my eyes up and down when I want to see distinctly far or near."

Ben called his new glasses "double spectacles." Today they aid the vision of thousands of people and are known as bifocals.

Sayings from POOR RICHARD'S ALMANACK

A saying is a simple, direct way of expressing a basic truth or piece of advice. Some of the sayings in this selection will be familiar to you, although you may not have known that they came from *Poor Richard's Almanack*. Others will be new.

Not all of the sayings were original with Ben. He took them from many different sources — other writers, and the folk wisdom of Spain, France, Germany, England, and Wales. But he reworded most of the sayings in line with his rule that good writing should be "smooth, clear, and short."

- Fish and visitors smell in three days.
- God helps them that help themselves.
- Keep your eyes wide open before marriage, half shut afterwards.
- Three may keep a secret if two of them are dead.
- The rotten apple spoils his companions.
- It is hard for an empty sack to stand upright.
- Early to bed and early to rise makes a man healthy, wealthy, and wise.
- Men and melons are hard to know.
- He that goes a-borrowing, goes a-sorrowing.
- Creditors have better memories than debtors.
- Little strokes fell great oaks.
- Lost time is never found again.
- Be slow to choose a friend — slower in changing.
- If you would be loved, love and be lovable.
- Love your neighbor, yet don't pull down your hedge.
- An apple a day keeps the doctor away.
- God heals and the doctor takes the fee.
- A lie stands on one leg, the truth on two.
- It is ill manners to silence a fool, and cruelty to let him go on.
- He that lieth down with dogs shall rise up with fleas.
- To lengthen thy life, lessen thy meals.
- Never leave that till tomorrow which you can do today.
- The greatest talkers are the least doers.
- Nothing is certain but death and taxes.
- A mob's a monster — heads enough, but no brains.
- There never was a good war or a bad peace.
- The way to secure peace is to be prepared for war.
- The doors of wisdom are never shut.

Historic Sites
ASSOCIATED WITH BENJAMIN FRANKLIN

Many places linked with Benjamin Franklin can be found in the two cities where he spent most of his life: Boston and Philadelphia.

The house at 17 Milk Street in Boston where Franklin was born has long since been torn down. But the graves of Franklin's parents can still be seen in Boston's Old Granary Burial Ground, near the graves of Paul Revere, John Hancock, and Elizabeth VerGoose, who is thought to have written *Mother Goose*.

There are many more places connected with Franklin in Philadelphia, the city to which he came as a youth. Here are descriptions of the most important ones.

Independence Hall

Visitors to the birthplace of American liberty can look into the Assembly Room, where delegates to the Second Continental Congress, Ben Franklin among them, adopted the Declaration of Independence on July 4, 1776.

Eleven years later, a different group of delegates met in the same room to frame a Constitution for the United States. Once again Ben Franklin was there, a delegate from the state of Pennsylvania.

Franklin Court

This site is a few blocks from Independence Hall. It combines a grassy courtyard, an underground museum, and three historic houses that Franklin built in 1786, shortly after his return from France. The courtyard occupies the spot where Franklin's demolished home and printing shop once stood. Below the courtyard, in the underground museum, visitors can pick up a phone and hear what any of 47 famous people had to say about Franklin. On a sunken stage, doll-size puppets of Ben and other historic figures portray "Franklin on the World Stage."

Nearby, in one of three historic houses, is the Printing Office and Bindery, where you can see colonial methods of printing and bookmaking in action. Beyond that is the Benjamin Franklin Post Office, which commemorates Franklin's tour of duty as Deputy Postmaster General of the colonies.

The Franklin Institute Science Museum

Named for Benjamin Franklin, Philadelphia's largest science museum houses the Benjamin Franklin National Memorial. Here you can view exhibits of Ben's personal possessions and science artifacts that convey the scope of his accomplishments. It's the largest collection of Franklin memorabilia to be found anywhere. Benjamin Franklin's birthday is celebrated at the Science Museum each year with a grand "Birthday Bash" on the weekend closest to January 17.

The Benjamin Franklin Bust

This 16-foot-high bust of Franklin stands on Arch Street, just a block from where Franklin is buried in the Christ Church Burial Ground. The statue was made from 80,000 copper pennies, most of which were donated by Philadelphia schoolchildren. The coins symbolize one of Franklin's best-known sayings: "A penny saved is a penny earned."

Christ Church and its Burial Ground

Christ Church, founded in 1659, was the birthplace of the Protestant Episcopal Church in the United States. Franklin and his wife, Deborah, are buried next to one another in the church's quiet and peaceful burial ground. The cemetery is not open to the public, but Ben Franklin's grave is clearly visible through an openwork fence. There are always pennies on it. According to a local tradition, tossing a penny on Ben's grave will bring a person good fortune.

Bibliography AND SOURCE NOTES

The following books were especially helpful in my research for this biography.

The Autobiography and Other Writings by Benjamin Franklin, edited and with an introduction by Peter Shaw (New York: Bantam Books, 1982). Franklin's autobiography was written in four parts over a period of more than 17 years. The first part, which he wrote in 1771 during his second stay in England, only carries the story up to his marriage to Deborah Read in 1730, when Franklin was twenty-four. He resumed work on the *Autobiography* 13 years later, in 1784, while serving as ambassador to France, but wrote only a single chapter.

After his retirement and return to America, Franklin picked up the *Autobiography* again in 1788. But ill health and his duties at the Constitutional Convention kept him from devoting his full attention to the manuscript. At the time of his death, in 1790, he had only brought the chronicle up to 1757 and the beginning of his stay in London as the representative of the Pennsylvania colony.

The parts of the *Autobiography* that I found most interesting are those in which Franklin describes his youth in Boston, his running away to Philadelphia, and his early successes as a printer, journalist, and businessman.

In contrast to the *Autobiography*, Thomas Fleming's *The Man Who Dared the Lightning: A New Look at Benjamin Franklin* (New York: William Morrow and Company, Inc., 1971) offers a comprehensive and insightful picture of Franklin's entire life. Fleming places particular emphasis on Franklin's complicated relationship with his son, William.

Carl Sandburg's Pulitzer-prize-winning biography, *Benjamin Franklin* (New York: Penguin Books, 1991), is an incredibly thorough portrait of Franklin. No detail concerning the man and his activities appears to have escaped Sandburg's notice.

On the other hand, Catherine Drinker Bowen's *The Most Dangerous Man in America* doesn't pretend to be thorough. Its subtitle, *Scenes from the Life of Benjamin Franklin*, lets the reader know what to expect: glimpses of Franklin in action as he experiments with electricity, formulates a plan to unite the colonies, and stands up for America in Britain's House of Commons.

Two collections of Franklin's sayings and satiric writings helped me to appreciate the man's wisdom and his never-failing sense of humor. They are *The Wit and Wisdom of Benjamin Franklin* by James C. Humes (New York: HarperCollins Publishers, 1995) and *Fart Proudly: Writings of Benjamin Franklin You Never Read in School*, edited by Carl Japikse (Columbus, Ohio: Enthea Press, 1990).

For help in compiling the list of historic sites associated with Franklin, I turned to three excellent travel guides: *A Guide's Guide to Philadelphia* by Julie Curson (Philadelphia: Curson House, Inc., 1991), *Frommer's Guide to Philadelphia & the Amish Country* by Jay Golan (New York: Macmillan USA, 1999), and *Uncommon Boston* by Susan and Jill Bloom (Reading, Massachusetts: Addison-Wesley Publishing Company, 1990).

I also benefited greatly from several trips I made to Philadelphia during the course of the research. There I revisited Independence Hall, explored Franklin Court, and was given a tour of the American Philosophical Society, which Franklin founded. In the Society's library, I saw one of the few existing portraits of Deborah Franklin and watched as a guide demonstrated how Franklin's ingenious library chair worked.

—*J.C.G.*
MAY 1999

Artist's Note

Capturing Benjamin Franklin's long and colorful life in pictures required an enormous amount of research. In order to do this, I had to find references to accurately depict all of the places, objects, backgrounds, characters, and costumes from Franklin's world.

I began my research at the Printing Office and Bindery at 4th and Market Street in Philadelphia. There I learned about the printing press and the printing process that was used in Franklin's time.

As a young apprentice, Ben would have had to learn how to set type. At that time, there were no keyboards. Putting printed words to paper in the days before computers or typewriters was a tedious process. Each metal letter had to be individually placed by hand — backward and upside down. On page 43 I have shown Franklin's name depicted in these hand-set letters.

Ben would also have been responsible for dipping the ink balls into the ink and pressing them down onto the set type. This process would transfer the ink onto the type. On page 10, I've depicted Ben carrying ink balls to the press. In the same picture, his brother is standing by the tympan, the upright board that holds the paper down onto the type. The printer would pull a lever across the printing press, forcing the paper down onto the inked type. The printing press shown here and on the cover is called a Caslon Old English Printing Press, named for the style of type it used. With this machine, some printing offices of the colonial period could print up to 2,000 pieces of literature a day.

I also did research at the American Philosophical Society, a library that was started by Franklin himself. There, Mr. Roy Goodman, the curator, was instrumental in helping me research Franklin's life down to the last detail — from how old Franklin was when he wore glasses to what the tax stamp and *The Pennsylvania Gazette* looked like.

For further research, I traveled to places where I could see history come alive. I viewed a reenactment of a Revolutionary War battle, the Battle of Brandywine, and toured Williamsburg, Virginia. I explored Philadelphia's Independence Hall and Elfreth's Alley and many other colonial sites. I also delved into every history book I could find on the subject. I had to know what type of wigs and clothes were worn, what a colonial carriage or ship looked like, and whether a certain type of chair was appropriate for that time period. By reading numerous historical accounts, I was able to answer these and many other questions.

Family and friends were called on to pose for me in costume. At times, I even modeled myself — changing my face and body type to suit a particular character. In fact, I modeled for all the men eating at the table on page 7!

To develop a character or a scene, I like to use the illustration to weave a second emotional line into the story. For example, page 28 shows the colonial men marching off to war as a little girl clutches her mother's leg. The girl is never mentioned in the text. The words simply say: "The Revolutionary War... had begun." By injecting such touches, I try to create a mood or to show how people, like the little girl, would have felt about the situation.

Ben's life was so rich, so long, and so varied. How do you illustrate 84 years of someone's life in 48 pages? The possibilities were overwhelming. Hence, I found it necessary to leave some things up to the imagination — and to pull out just those scenes that I felt would not only tell Ben's story, but the story of colonial life as well.

M. Dooling

Index

(Page numbers in italics indicate illustrations.)